T0168519

MILK AND FILTH

Camino del Sol
A Latina and Latino Literary Series

MILK

FILTH

CARMEN GIMÉNEZ SMITH

THE UNIVERSITY OF
ARIZONA PRESS

TUCSON

The University of Arizona Press
© 2013 Carmen Giménez Smith

www.uapress.arizona.edu

Library of Congress Cataloging-in-Publication Data
Giménez Smith, Carmen, 1971–
[Poems. Selections]
Milk and filth / Carmen Giménez Smith.
pages ; cm. — (Camino del sol: a latina and latino literary series)
ISBN 978-0-8165-2116-6 (pbk. : acid-free paper)
I. Title.
PS3607.I45215M55 2013
811'.6—dc23

                              2013004661

Publication of this book is made possible in part by the proceeds of a permanent endowment
created with the assistance of a Challenge Grant from the National Endowment for the Human-
ities, a federal agency.

Manufactured in the United States of America on acid-free, archival-quality paper containing a
minimum of 30% post-consumer waste and processed chlorine free.

To Rosa Alcalá

CONTENTS

III. Becoming

ACKNOWLEDGMENTS

Many thanks to the editors who published these poems, some in different forms, in the following publications: "Malinché," "And the Mouth Lies Open," and "Something New" in *The Acentos Review*; "Diving into the Spoil" (as "Known to the River") in *Chicago Review*; "Radicalization" in *delirious hem*; "For Lars Von Trier," "Feminine Agency," and "Rosy Complexion" in *The Equalizer*; "Juicy Couture" in *H_NGM_N*; "Fragments from the Confessions" in *jubilat*; "Phaedra" (as "Oracular"), "The Red Lady," "Deluxe and Amply-Rewarded Juliette," and part of "And the Mouth Lies Open" (as "Glass Calliope") in *No Tell Motel*; "Happy Trigger" in *Tuesday; An Art Project*; "Our Tiny Dimensions" in *Whiskey Train*; and "Parts of an Autobiography" in *Evening Will Come*. "Can We Talk Here," "Lolita Archetype," and portions of "Parts of an Autobiography" (as "Of Beauty") appeared in the chapbook *Can We Talk Here,* published by Belladonna Books in 2011.

MILK AND FILTH

HAPPY TRIGGER

Off-season and in
the burnt forest
of my nightgown, a feral
undergrowth that marks
me as burial site—
to be still enough or
just enough.

My arms become fat arms:
hearth. I eat dirt for doubt,
a secret bleached
old as lie. I out-want
like a spindly
winged monster.
If I were a bug—
were I—then you'd hope
for reparation, and paint
more brown into the plot.

I

GENDER FABLES

(MALINCHÉ)

The native is shorn of the coarse,

then cloaked in a brocade ellipsis. She figures

this a better vocation

than the other thing, the desert chingadera.

They tell her, *you're too good for rancheros, and*

for the volcano veneration shill melted into fetters,

but she gets banished for her valor.

Her first translation:

"This speech fills our gaps with Civilization, with

my misprision. It sets wild into new fluencies."

Her sisters surround her and she asks,

They boil the goat's tongue and then what is it?

She tells them she plans to inter our dialect

into theirs, our divinity. She wants mongrel dictions

to add to her arsenal. She wants to be lord.

(FRAGMENTS FROM THE CONFESSIONS)

Take the jar and crack it open.

The jar is a plaster cast of my down

there, so take that jar to the end

of a tunnel. Defile that jar, burn it,

tag it. Venerate it with dung and Sappho.

Don't hang my jar over me. *It's my jar, it's my jar!*

Decoupage the jar with mouths

cut from *Cosmo*, mister death,

fill it with our minstrel blood

or the placenta from our collective lacunae.

Grow lascivious magnolias in it,

heavy-lipped and lush with pollen.

The jar houses my illusions

of eating men like hairballs.

(LLORONA SOLILOQUY)

The river's dried up once made of my hair

I've left behind rubble but it's thinking

of all of us that I make a tiny baby funeral

of my tears and they make me a reason

for beatings so I had better find the thing

I left behind since it was precious

like the plaza where I used to throw coins

and wish for someplace else to be like the shimmer

of coins in water that newness not the borne-down

appendage like the body is haven as passageway

to life I make to death because it's easier

in the long term shadow of this body and its vacuum

(WIZARDINE)

The charlatan was prelude
to the fracas I'd be.
Oh, those razor-sharp
appetites and their audacious
hullabaloo.

Once two modes diverged
on that yellow path.
One was surgical theatre,
the other a populist
allegory about shoes
and some witch and her sister.

I fell for his conjury,
flapped out the old trousseau
mother had also set
in my cigar box. Not just
the suggestion of virtue
but the bona fide bastille
wrapped in plastic.

We met in the shadow
of his artificial interrogation
and wrested out the victories
from each other's defects.

(GUERILLA ROMEOS)

They built a tent city

on the periphery of Sodom,

moved by idealism and

the spectacle of a briefer Fall.

They were driven out by vigilantes

who threw rocks at the window.

Someone get a broom

for the broken tabernacle.

What to do, what to do with

the raw assembly line of pillars?

Mistaking it for the flood,

the squandered daughters

flee with all their new wealth,

fecundity, and hollow,

vanity and thanatos:

ingenious how they skirted taboo.

(AND THE MOUTH LIES OPEN)

The wave comes down,

so duck under for its smother,

each is a planet to colonize:

the one with hotels,

the one with plotting old

women in an apocalyptic

debtors' prison. Classic fiction

is colossal ruse, the site of Ponzi

fraud. Please note how much it costs

to be muse: the toll of influence,

cases and cases of Dom Pérignon,

full-body depilation and the most

lavish immortality unguents online.

Clothes that are maybe too young

for me, and the attendant mortification,

fake brunches. I pay for affirmation

from a woman in a white noise office who

guides me through behavior modification

and trauma, yet I'm still only a morsel

of authority: my print is barely detectable

in the camber of the canon for which

I gave my egos and my wits. I'm a nervous

fiasco if only for your sanction.

My alternate reality is a dimension

where a psychiatrist stares dumb

at my bosom while we talk about

drowning in the suds of dish rags.

In this other one, I don't ever

discover the compulsion

of verbal cunning. I'm a science

fiction movie and electrocution

makes me a Frankenbride

in Technicolor abjection.

(PHAEDRA)

I needed flight, so I called

to the gods, then remembered I was atheist.

I gave my virtue to a son, but he threw it

to the ground. The rock star was my weakness,

but I got stuck in his drum solo.

I needed flight, collected feathers and candles,

but the assembly required measure—

not like the myth—and a type of daring

I didn't possess. I landed in a bed of cloud,

still requiring flight, a transcendence

I read about in someone else's poem,

and I wished I were that poem,

that poet, but I was not of that school.

I rolled pennies and quarters into

paper sleeves for the first flight out of limbo.

I tried to buy a drink, but the steward

told me I was too wasted on hubris.

We flew in a plane that split open

like tin over an ocean that folded us

into its animal ferocity. Shark chattel,

another flight, but now water's matter:

a gallivant into the caustic domain of urchins

where the golden sun-apple swans me,

taps my root, mourns my velvet,

messengers me. Doodly-do,

I'm useless. Watch me suffocate.

(THE MIND READER ADVISES GUADALUPE)

You fly into your tasks, supernatural queen,

but your transgressions bind you to limbo.

You cling to strife because the colonizing

worm is buried deep in you and wouldn't you

know who came to define you? Fate is irony.

You're technically childless, exempt mother,

more bound to blood ritual than your kin,

yet this work satisfies you. You'd like to downgrade

into human. Then what? Amorality, osteoporosis

and not even a marble estuary for the ages.

(THE RED LADY)

You blissfully walk her
plank to the apex
of collusion. She welts
skin with a name tattoo.
The ocean's salt
is tender sedative.
The blade was made
in the furnace where
excess is made and tiger
and where we sleep
like vampires when God
comes knocking.
She constructs a man
limb by limb from the earth,
and he belongs to us,
so we tear him apart
because he belongs to us.
You leave cloud
out of your play because
he's amateur, because his mouth
does nothing for her vacancies.
No one dares mutiny the force
from the red, her eyes, the dress.
Soul showed his,
and Captain slathered him
and converged upon his
flesh, ripe with female climate.

(DELUXE AND AMPLY-REWARDED JULIETTE)

The Pope invents nihilism, and then Juliette is born.

She gets wrapped in gossamer, sent away,

then liberated through submission,

then cut, then spit, then subjected.

Bound to her excess by history,

we acquire the blood lease of her body

through her deference to utopian carnival

(our libido is constructed this way).

I can barely see her. Heavy with aura,

a libertine's hazard, she's a visionary's

invitation to nadir, faceless and dilated.

[SUSANNAH'S NOCTURNE]

When deep, I hated the weed hands,

and weed hair. I hated down

to the very granular residence.

That flesh was no true relation

to mine. Pink and peeling,

fresh out of mist, I rose from the place

they pulled me down from and into the Bible.

I got to calling it Before and After,

then put a latch on the gate for tomorrow.

I became the gelatin shiver of tea's

surface, that spent emotion.

On the bank hatching fable,

looking for the other though

the other was Me. I freed myself

through tree music, what some called

my morality-inflicted wound.

More to the story that I can't get inside

or out of without rope. In both

the story and the trope, I am bride.

Not musical, this body. Not chorus.

Secession was the only option.

My currency's spent, death's ironic
scraping of walls, skin on resistant skin.
We should link our arms around all bodies
of water because they are all our waters.

(LOLITA ARCHETYPE)

Heroine breaks through better-late-than-never-dreams
of pushing his legs back and poking at aperture.

Her older brothers used to dare her to hold her
hand over a lit flame. They learned when to pull away
while it was still good enough to not lose face,
but she let the flame peel away at the skin of her palm.

In the right light, you can see scar.
Her metaphorical hymen like a hermetic seal.

She was the cream of his crop.
Her hips looked occupied, even with clothes on.

Front room of his house: big windows
decorated with Xmas lights and old
cobwebs and a wife's notion of hominess.

The drive there is silent. He brushes her leg
with a lazy fingernail. The heroine is on vacation.
Qualifications and heights get her there.
He tells her she reminds him of the girls
he dreamt of when he was young: the Playboy
girls with dark hair and gypsy beads.
They were always called Lola.

Symmetry, her liver color, the asp that killed
Cleopatra, a Beardsley print of two young men at each other,
the smell of her deeper than a conch,
liquid as record. We're a tangle of contracts.

(HYSTERIA)

That there's a hex don't vex.
Sometimes it's scales or void.
The lyre plies with division
and a predicament is born.
Demeter became monster,
foul shame to motherhood.
We can be so insensitive
with others' losses when
they aren't our losses.

(BABA YAGA)

Because she's better-suited for unsolvable

Old World type villainy, I venerate

her in a story. Each time, she wants

breathtaking, but she gets buttered by the forest

tree's diffident reach instead. Turbulence

coming at her from the center of the ahistorical

spire. She's of kohl eye, greasy darkness.

Night's blight takes the total human from her.

II
SMALL DEATHS

DIVING INTO THE SPOIL

Down in the ocean's blur:

green sediment root.

In the fathoms, we're wiped away.

The map tattooed

on our flanks is more

immanence than fish

or the weeds.

The hives embody

the ambition of all

our descents.

We find a busted lock

on the hive spoilt

by salt and barnacle.

The treasures

are vermilion

and yellow scripts

that deduce

the foul old

compass's course.

We find idiom
to tell our daughter
how every woman's
heart swims with searching.

       Who begat the hives?
she asks.

We slipped out of the water,
and the hives were gone.
Fish heart: water is bitter
on its account.
A fish hung round our neck.

EPIPHANY AT LA CUEVA

Soaring like a startled flock
out of the shelter of trees,

I felt what mother earth was about:
the daughter with the scabbed leg,

the flinty wall of the mountain
and my tenuous hold on it all.

A dispatch from the Bernhardian
force field of dread, I called it.

Trees, caverns, rocks
made perilous by green.

EPIGRAMS FOR A LADY

If you hate it when your son is preternaturally boy, freight him with your trunk's warp.

A woman could form a bastion with a man, but for it to persist, both parties must wield Kalashnikovs and permission from Uber-Mom.

The idiot, the bad apple: the same thing as prototypical feminine.

The best enemy against antagonism is more howl and less whisper.

Frizz and anxiety are not kin but married by the friction they arouse in us.

She who does not know how to put her business on the streets ought not to enter the art biz.

One is often punished for her lavish disregard of easy permissions.

The breadth of a woman's sexuality reaches into the accidental pinnacle of our collective wit.

A woman's egg is the reason she does not easily give herself to death/sex drive.

Self-loathing as apparatus: 100 years of hindrance.

What is done out of fear smells like devotion and patriarchy.

Frequently, the slattern is not the equal of her crime. She slanders herself needlessly, especially if/when/because no one is watching. Be patient. For once, the supplicant masses await your gap.

QUEENLY

The bell's chain is held back
from striking against wonderment
by the angel's heavy hand.
The angel represents ruin.
The decline of me
got started in the coiled heart
of old wives tales, nightmares
of history. A woman can't
hold all that storm in her head,
so she surrenders to it.

FOR LARS VON TRIER

This is a gesture of offense but not meant
offensively: *I'd like to garrote you with your*
camera as an in-kind spectacle.

Ideological chirping keeps culture in the business
of throwing bricks. The way you're obsessed is
au courant with warriors.

Revelations are vibrant when awash
in the tears of babies, in the sweat of witches.
I'm with you on dystopia, but not martyrdom.

Your scholars are narrow and red-eyed. They
divine marriage sacraments from your
data and prospect three paradigms out of your oeuvre.

They are:
1. The finale should be a blast of sacrifice.
2. The sacrifice is erotic mouth, sewn open up to the eyes.
3. One digs up the mis-tolds and dresses them in 3-D awe.

RADICALIZATION

An agitator holds her sign up asking *do you feel equal,*
so you and your sisters deride her
because she's so public about injustice, so
second-wave. Your sisters gather around

her with scorn and sully her earnest nature. It's
thanks but no thanks. I can vote,
walk into the pharmacy for my Plan B, and wear
a chain wallet. One sister throws an apple

into the melee and the unfazed agitator bites it.
Her straight block-teeth break
the fruit apart which shocks your
sisters, but when they've abandoned their mockery

for the lure of a choice bazaar—earrings, Ugg boots,
removable tramp stamps,
a *Sex and the City* marathon—you're *hot* for
the agitator. The crowd clears and you kiss

her sweaty neck and use her agitating sign as a bed.
You scrawl her agitating words
onto your belly and stand naked against
her muscle memory. Not just the cause,

the impulse, the result, but the buzz

of lack. You'd like to consume it right

out of her, that humming electric

dissatisfaction. Then you'd like to put it

out of your body in the form

of a Louise Bourgeois sculpture, milky,

blobbing, love the star-fuckery

of doing it with her and to her, then

the sticky pulling apart,

the eternal production

of polyurethane eggs

wrapped in yarn.

PARTS OF AN AUTOBIOGRAPHY

1. My mother was a cater-waiter. She wrote rubber checks that kept our dysfunction afloat. She didn't cook or do windows.

2. Her life was difficult *because* she was a brown woman. This was and is indisputable.

3. She taught me to braid a rope of my hair out of the abyss of our class, poems for ascension.

4. She gave me androgyny when I was trying to defy category.

5. Or: the rules were out of my reach.

6. In college I was groomed to overthrow patriarchy by the capri-panted rebel who introduced me to *Our Bodies, Ourselves* in my first women's studies class who taught us about the number thirteen and the Venus of Willendorf. This was in the late '80s and early '90s.

7. She encouraged me to read scholarly feminist texts, which led me to Simone de Beauvoir. After that I fell in love with Dworkin's mordant critique of seventies porn and Rich's takedown of the homosocial. This coterie of muses on my shoulder was as outraged as I was.

8. I suffered with unbridled optimism and signed on at the Women's Resource Center and began using "his or her" in my papers.

9. I saw my cervix during a Pap smear.

10. The whole world had a new layer of grime for me to pick at: misogyny.

11. I decided my eggs were my own commodity.

12. Eager to expand my newly-minted wisdom, I pored over books of anti-essentialism and feminist separatism to find the answer that would disentangle the question mark/speculum that had formed my path.

13. Feminism tried to accommodate me inside of its confines when I was a polygon.

14. Sometimes feminism seemed a miracle, a cork bobbing up for air in the ocean.

15. Or I was the cork and the ocean was everything else that conspired and conspires to be like a cage.

16. I was young and easily astonished, stunned, insulted. I was often subsumed by the vagaries of my sex, and this remains a source.

17. When I first began writing poetry, first began thinking of poetry, I was certain that I could rely on the I/eye, which turned out to be the most elusive quality.

18. *So squeezed, wince you I scream? I love you and hate off with you.*

19. Sylvia Plath's work gave me synaesthetic pleasure. The speaker's self-mortification perverted the edges of all her lines with sweetish vinegar.

20. Her poetry was pungent when so little poetry is pungent. Poetry of regimented epiphany smelled like fabric softener when I was young.

21. I liked my poetry to smell like I had forgotten my deodorant. You could smell me from across the table. I liked my work to smell of work and fuck.

22. I wanted to make bloody holes in the earth with my body like Ana Mendieta, but with poems.

23. That was when I was young, but it's still true now.

24. I saw power and its limited scope, and I wanted it.

25. This want created a monster, a feminist.

26. I'm a feminist for all the bodies strewn over history and semi-emerging from the earth.

27. There are deserted bodies and ruined bodies and starved bodies all around me.

28. My mother's body once was sharp. Now, it's delusional and rotten with dementia.

29. My baby sister killed her body and other girls have destroyed their bodies since then.

30. I write angry that these women had little agency in this world and that they are not in books.

31. This anger requires that I adapt the tenets of my feminist aspiration. Saving the world for decaying female bodies, for example.

32. What I will do with power might terrify.

33. Anyone can enter my work because it's about viscera, and I've got wounds into it and they're little windows into the workings of me.

34. The reveal: the *abject pleasure of this abject mind*.

35. I write a poem in which I reveal my true feelings. The body is the engine and the brain is the hindrance.

36. I silence the brain with language play. I also break down the sentence, accommodate my ample ass in it, neutralize the modification with it.

37. To write a poem, I mustn't be wearing a bra.

38. I'm debased, but not that low. I'm just more animal than machine, more heart than head.

39. I'm a worm with bones and a sophisticated sensing organ. I'm guts in a vise.

40. Scars are radical exposition. I'm provoked by the way scars encroach the body. I am working on a catalog of my scars.

41. Confessional implies shame, whereas a scar is the trace of violence and it's always connected to a narrative about the body and it is more than confession, perhaps emblem.

42. I kneel at confession and my knees bear the trace of my abasement, where the *action* is.

43. I'm a sophisticated sensing organ with stigmatized segments. That's my baser profile.

44. I don't pretend that I write solely because of beauty.

45. I love beauty in all its forms, innocence and decay, filth and jewels. Sometimes I write muttering mumbo jumbo for beauty.

46. My history with writing is a history with failure. Not elegant aesthetic failure, but fuck-up-failure like I have detention *for life*.

47. *I never got good at affecting the blank expression of truly contemporary beauty.*

48. These circumstances make me tragic and solipsistic. I'll wait until I get voted off of the island, but until then I'll continue to make.

49. *I live like a bourgeois and save my radical for art.* I'm scared of my childhood, radical in its ugliness and its flux.

50. That was one unenchanted childhood, yet I lived mostly in my imagination, so much is not faithfully recorded but rather made strange or grotesque in memory colored by imagination.

51. I am not a journalist.

52. That childhood is why I am a poet. I planned to chronicle it. I planned to make it cautionary and gut.

53. From my notebook: *I cannot imagine a sense of self that doesn't integrate all of the qualities my parents possess. Instead I buried it in smoke and the clay of metaphor and everyone confused it with static.*

54. I want my problems to be Wallace Stevens, but they're Anne Sexton.

55. I'll tell you one story: Broken, then put back together with soap.

56. A woman on a book review site calls me a bad mother, both disappointing and satisfying, as her description meant that I had portrayed myself accurately.

57. Her review requires her to reach for dichotomy, and I hope to always fall towards the problematic end because it's the truest.

58. I'm the Shitty Parent, I'm a Shitty Parent. I write my reparations but don't back off from the art. I'll be the one that teaches my children about complicated people.

59. The writing is not the catharsis. The decision to excavate is the catharsis. The transformation from dreadfulness to art is the catharsis, but the art is the art.

60. I'm saving it for the art is why. This is manifesto is why. Let's just say fugue-worthy.

61. I am not averse to working on myself in my art.

62. I want to make explosions in the air like Cai Guo-Quiang, except with letters.

63. Undoing the impulse to know the self through mind to instead learn the self through mortification.

64. Ana Mendieta does bloody and visceral and elemental things. She took her body and put it everywhere. She took her sex and put it everywhere. She bruised the earth with slits.

65. Ana Mendieta: *the empire at the end of decadence.*

66. Because her art is ephemeral, it gets recorded. Even the body, ephemeral, gets recorded.

67. Prescience.

68. To make something more of our traces. To garland the trees with clots of me.

69. *But here, covered by the earth whose prisoner I am, I feel death palpitating underneath the earth.*

70. The shame is there, but I'm not shamed or ashamed. The grander the failure, the more elaborate the word-shrine.

71. Off the leash.

72. I'm the Shitty Friend writing valentines. I modify everything.

73. I'm not a total cunt.

74. I write poems to Christine and to Krystal and to Lily and to Rosa and to Rachel and to Tawnya and to Aïda and Kari and Larisa and to Lety and to Courtney and Barbara.

75. I write paeans and apologies and analyses of our complex connections.

76. I write poems to them, and I write poems in which I am like them.

77. That they're heroes and bandits.

78. I'm writing to say that I'm sorry I didn't call back. I'm writing to say that they obsess me and inhabit me.

79. My Audience is private, but a true person. She is real flesh but a stranger to me.

80. You know how sometimes you want to be one kind of person, but you're that other kind of person? Like that.

81. I indict her of my sins.

82. I construct her, I revere her, I fold her in eighths, I burn her up.

83. *Or say what you meant, you coward . . . This baby that I bleed.*

84. I like the voice of certain poems, husky like Joni Mitchell's cigarette-ruined voice.

85. I like a poem that reminds me of the time I fell in love with poetry and the kind of poetry I was fed, which was unseasoned-quinoa-Sharon-Olds-esque.

86. I want pathos, bathos, and sinking in the viscosity of feeling. If I can make something lovely of my broken crockery, then I shall.

87. I am my baby sister's surviving twin, narrowly averting the piano from the window, and I will use that survival as tribute.

88. I don't understand dainty except when explained patiently.

89. Today I'd give great sums for a beautiful mouth or the knowledge of scarf artistry and how to deploy beauty as a weapon or as currency, as I've seen it done.

90. Because of how I was grown, I came to think women were either trimmed or untrimmed. Luminous vs. dim. Lush, flat. I'm of the latter, half-hearted and ham-fisted.

91. I'm of the latter, but with something to tap into.

92. If I write my body, what comes out is: ooohhh. Arch moon.

93. I'm a baby machine.

94. My mouths don't speak the same language.

95. My friend Jamie's mom was so nice when I went crazy in the '90s. To pay it forward.

96. Beauty is a desired illusion, performance. It lives just outside my reach, the bizarre type.

97. I want to stage a coup, mostly an aesthetic one borne out of my coarse tie to concept and my tender marriage to language.

98. *I walk beneath your pens, and am not what I truly am, but what you'd prefer to imagine me.*

99. I'll write screeds, manifestos and epilogues on the merits of female domination.

100. I would like to act in resistance to the classist assumptions of post-feminism. I would like to write about gender folded into race and class folded into gender too.

101. This coup will bring back the little bit didactic, the little bit ham-fisted because it'll be good for us.

102. This coup will be a collaboration of squabbling and seeing into the shared past to construct the shared future. I aestheticize all my struggles: complicated and as close to art, capital A, as I can do.

103. I like the crystalline tear like morning and climax with crying of language that overflows with afterbirth and rainbows and applause. *Those knock-out body fluids: blood, sperm, tears!*

104. Part-Césaire, part-Solanas, part blood-sweat-and-tears.

105. Part my mother and my sisters. My friends and my enemies and my frenemies, all their beautiful mouths.

106. As treatment. As caprice. As my femme-chivalry.

107. Some death and suicide. Bits of puppy dog tails and sticks-and-stones. Accents and neologisms with a slapdash you-just-wouldn't-understand.

108. For Yvonne.

109. Know what I have to do, but I don't do it.

110. As the sun and hell, as the serpent and as chaos, as the maw of many mouths.

111. Necessity is the mother of all that pours out of me.

TRIGGER WARNING

My drag is a kind of elevator.

It's like a title.

You're soaking in it.

It's a courtesy chainmail for your protection.

I start my stories with it,

and when I'm hungry, it opens the door.

The door is pop-up window into my soul.

Deep and meditative, a vertigo of soul.

My cruel, divisive temperament: my cross

to bear. We all bear it because of our

shared ancestry of milk and filth.

THE DAUGHTER

We said she was a negative image of me because of her lightness.

She's light and also passage, the glory in my cortex.

Daughter, where did you get all that goddess?

Her eyes are Neruda's two dark pools at twilight.

Sometimes she's a stranger in my home because I hadn't imagined her.

Who will her daughter be?

She and I are the gradual ebb of my mother's darkness.

I unfurl the ribbon of her life, and it's a smooth long hallway,

doors flung open.

Her surface is a deflection is why.

Harm on her, harm on us all.

Inside her, my grit and timbre, my reckless.

ESSENTIALISM

I bleed

you bleed or bled

connected

or dipped in blood

I have in me a dwelling

occupied

vacant or atrophied

all house

I tickle

you tickle

that spot

I lovely lady lumps

your lumps as lovely

voice boxes

sized approximately

bodies painted somewhere

somewhere painted

subject of painting

subject of subjectivity

see *Mad Love*

desecration fodder

penetration location

binary sense of E.R.A.

in the velvet hairs

of the neck

tips of adornment

unadorned tips

with potential

but tips all the same

me is a pastiche

of learned gesture

and you the same

with a different register

once or twice evacuated

or never evacuated

but that you can

the body evidence

and its variable story.

CAN WE TALK HERE

after Joan Rivers

My soul's myelin sheath is so tattered, even the tattoo of drumming fingernails makes me a fundamentalist.

I have no sugar left after forty. If my husband wasn't twisted and starved, we might never turn our sex into text.

My parents can't describe me. All they ever see is assimilation and coconut. All they say is, "Why can't you just build yourself a Trojan horse into the big league?"

My first marriage killed itself, but it was my fault. We were playing house and then I took the bag off my face, revealing Mina Loy in housewife-drag.

Before I write poems, the laptop takes a pain killer.

Poetry has more holes than Swiss. Hole-y and pale yellow and sliced in markets.

Our system is so broken, I break for commercials before the Q and A.

I blame white privilege for my poor sense of self. All they tell me is "This small cell will be your pasture." For twenty years I built a key from the shrapnel in my head.

I write flabby poems, but fortunately my smart bombs cover them.

I knew I was an unwanted visitor to the paradigm parade when I saw that my gift basket included nuance and a muzzle.

I told Poet X that this house was our house and he said, "The boat awaits your olive complexion, but that's just white persona talking."

I wish I was a clone, so I could know what I'd look like without the imbroglio.

Is poetry fat? Let's just say that second helpings of unpolitic irony is a buffet.

My body is so distended from being vessel and highway; I barely notice the husband's invasion until the leak and the hiss.

SOMETHING NEW

You have to want the induction of marriage
with its lot of glue along with its half-death,
helmets with initials carved in,
persnickety daughters demanding liberal nods,
half-baked urbaniacs living on Main and Third
disposed to codependent students who jam
the worn-through study to ask
how to proportion language beyond light,
mortgages dangling your bit
of check balance out to dry.

You have to want to cry in Kansas,
that dark theater, and worry with the pills
your health would find:
descending a staircase to a spouse with wild hair
and drops of spit on his/her hairshirt, the garden
pecked over by birds. You'd have to
want it because there's another place where
it's air-conditioned and dark and upholstered
and slattern and lush and devout, a place
of libidinous blackout. You'd have to really want it.

ROSY COMPLEXION

Spasms, deliriums: madness is such a female world, but that's just my take.

Failing often and long at it, I do claim to know girls are there for blame.

You too can be matter, purplish and pale: the universe's chasm.

I noticed you when you got lustier by calling down a blood spell.

Cleanliness is only a necessity in hospitals, is what I teach my daughter.

She will be filthy.

I am plain. I was plain. I will be plain. I am not, though.

My bad habits are secrets, the mention of secrets, going to the last chapter first.

I do nothing with my urges because they are manufactured urges.

YOUR DATA IS POLITICAL

Your presence rises from scavenging: pages and words

and webs and signs. You've become a target but without

the old spy store gadgets. I'd like to know what you know,

not just your count. I click on you, then you click back,

precious darling surface. We add, poke, text.

On my iPhone, you're called The Outlier.

Your profile pic of a yellow vase

is so allusory, so art, or your skirt flips up and you're viral,

or someone else outs you as the double-crossing wife

because it's Old West open season on Facebook.

Pages ripple with alacrity, with betrayal and Outlook keeps

the other engine purring and sneaky. Two presences.

The real and the fable vanish before you and to them

within barcode, a cornucopia of insight

(a family's fleecing, caravans of product, blurry pirated video).

I'll play Sarah McLachlan over your visage, elegiac, or someone

will paste your face onto the porno performance artist

baptized with secretion. I'll be the cultural anxiety,

and you can be the Luddite. We'll be a perfect pairing

of antediluvian (the wine) and digital (the host).

OUR TINY DIMENSIONS

The body's measure is our way.

The archetype narrowed and no one winced.

We want something that doesn't exist

anymore because of biology.

We want taut but get density, flour.

The measure of organs is our way.

We talk about it with strangers and should be ashamed.

We're planning the three tips that can shrink us.

We're holding our ankles hostage with a measuring tape:

against it, bound to the tape.

I want to turn myself into an infant. You want to be plinth.

We're figures. We're lists of expenditure and food diaries,

but today I held the middle of me in hand and shook it.

It shook, shook like something fun.

OVOID

A gathering of cells,

thrumming

roundness,

potential

humming fondness.

No big event firstly.

Traced with two threads,

in a meeting of matter.

Body infests the Body.

Biology: to fight

or reject or construct

impasse.

Sharp and shielding

fluid, detonation

though sometimes petrified

or distorted. Useless.

Chasm irritant,

or miracle, a new trope

of replicate, of embodied

communion and captivity.

JUICY COUTURE

Make my clothes dripping,

and make them organ and smoke.

Make me an outfit with mutable bloom,

an envy magnet. Make

me a fabric that changes

the subject. Truss me like a bottle

filled with artificial blue or red

to suit my character, full of holes

to suggest suggestion. I'd like

transport but also love bucket

and disputed borders.

LABOR DAY

I split open like a melon.
I bled and shat. My back was
semicolon. I bled and shat.
My sister-midwives rubbed me,
coaxed me. My husband held me up.
I bled and shat. I pushed so much,
I was inside out. From closed bud
to gaping, dying rose, petal by petal.
Layers of pearl built around a granule
of waste, the diamond ring clanging
in the pipes, the plunge of meconium
and blood, I shat and bled.

FEMININE AGENCY

We all want to divine adoration from the sky's ciphers,

but chain ourselves to the accuracy of rom-coms instead.

Self gets glossy with narcissism.

Self gets glossy with the city's isolation.

The door swings open as if we were

free, but it's a trick meant to remind us they've got the keys.

So they found out what we were and they plundered.

When does history become a scar? *Can't outgrow us, world.*

We're the real deal reads our slogan.

Promise is already a liar's kiss and a canceled check.

Pity—a foregone conclusion.

Sorry you can't locate the political occasion.

This is the *new* hunger strike.

A note on the door might make us stranger

again if we dared broadside the place.

Witness Protection: invent a new truculent

and gape-mouthed self with doors

into second-wave resurrection.

We take orientalism and make an unattainable girl of it.

BECOMING

A DEVIL INSIDE ME

after Ana Mendieta

1.

Seven Powers,

ye who are so sticky with our divine

effusions, I kneel in thee

with great piety

and exploit your intercession

through the Great Spirit.

See my petition and grant

me agency and vision.

Please remove

any obstacle that causes

me to stray from the Beauty Way.

Olofi, I trust

in the words "the personal

is political." Let it be so.

2 .

Art had a problem.

Her body was explicit

abattoir with its ribbons

of sulfurous smoke

and raw animus. Her body

was a meteor,

but wasn't being written.

Press a hand into

earth's flesh—

duplexity comes up

like inception.

The bodyprint

is an illegible surge:

of leaving trace

of self en route.

The figure

like a bottle of wine,

stiff as a board, grave

as lead. What moves

underneath? The moss

silhouette, mute but vatic.

3 .

Inside the thicket, the tree.

Inside the tree, heart.

Inside heart,

the water where body garlands

the surface like fur.

The body, a territory.

From inside the territory,

call for reversal. The call

for reversal is native, first.

4 .

Water encloses

the body's vestige

in a conspiracy

of sticks, or the body

schemes with verdure

and mud ambrosia,

in a tree trunk,

that baptismal consecration.

Art history banished

the body and its sopping glut in

customary expulsion.

The body pushes back.

She is found *embedded*, heart *exuded*

in the wind, the study, in stone

outcroppings, in land, marvel.

Torrent of impulse,

torrent of unlikeliness.

Implacable corpse in

the aesthetic mortuary.

And for this she brought

the process of gunpowder.

For this work, audience

and documentation

from every vista, each atom

as witness and cohort.

5.

Because she's marginalized in situ,

she stitches hairs to her face—

her squinting mug

is coarse mistress parody.

Bloodied mortification and witness

makes her work marianism.

Raised in paper houses

and their attendant infiltration,

immersed in these new reclamations,

she strips the land of its nationalist

fripperies for scrap metal.

6.

The body is a battleground. Drone attacks

on it. If it's broken, they buy it.

If it's splayed on the table

for dissection, they bought it. Blood

is the enterprise. The rocket

in their pocket is a passport. The wind

tucks the ash into its pulsing. To seize that

force and dam up the rivers with it and furrow

the earth with an atoning blood-cure

and rise up into a storm to divide the sky—

real prayer woven in the threads.

7.

It's natal.

No hesitation.

She was brought up alien.

Arbiter of corpus release,

and root transience.

The crevasse effect craters

into mistranslated exoticism.

Maps aren't the discourse for it.

The theme of long-haired rosary

wipes out that old sovereignty.

Automaton just never felt right,

neither did provincial white goddess.

The traces of fervor in the very

ventricles of the conjoined earths.

The terrain is dark asylum,

positive darkness. Naturally, mutilation.

8 .

Why this kingdom?
You find the stone on a mountain
fit with others like it.
Not trees houses, villages, or wells.
This empire is disappeared.
Only seldom voices, stones with hours
tethered to them. The goddess is dead
from treason, so her people fade white
as water in the cold,
then disappear into the stone horizon,
become the wall's face.

WHEN GOD WAS A WOMAN

When God was a woman,
empire was *meh*.
When God was a woman,
we built Schools of Listening
and every week we sat quietly
until we could hear
each other's thoughts.

No shadows when God
was a woman. Little girls
had great dominion,
and grandmothers
were venerated.
Sky was the giant
bellows of her inside.

The grace of God meant
flowing and willowy. This
was when God was a woman.

She played harmless pranks
because she liked keeping
things light. She made it rain
on our collective good hair days.
When she met someone

who seemed fun

and a little mysterious, she invited

him into heaven,

then she made her daughter

blind for a week, which in retrospect

was kind of mean, but her

daughter made the best of it.

NOTES

"Gender Fables": This series is influenced, in part, by Cindy Sherman and Claude Cahun.

"Phaedra": The line "I'll watch you . . . suffocate" is from the Imogen Heap song, "Useless."

"The Red Lady" refers to the notorious sixteenth-century English female pirate whose identity has never been discovered. This poem is dedicated to Roberto Harrison and J. Michael Martinez.

"Susannah's Nocturne": The phrases "death's ironic scraping" and "spent emotion" are from Wallace Stevens's poem "Peter Quince at the Clavier."

In the poem "Hysteria," the quote "foul shame to motherhood" is attributed to Helen Hunt Jackson.

"Diving into the Spoil": The poem is an adaptation of the Adrienne Rich poem "Diving into the Wreck," and contains pieces of my poem "Known to the River," which was published in *Chicago Review*.

"Parts of an Autobiography":
"So squeezed . . . hate off with you." John Berryman
"abject pleasure . . . Abject mind." Juvenal
"I never got good . . . contemporary beauty." Ariana Reines
"Those . . . sperm, tears!" Jean Genet
"Or say what . . . This baby that I bleed." Anne Sexton
"I live like . . . radical for art." Gustave Flaubert
"the empire . . . decadence." Paul Verlaine
"But here . . . underneath the earth." Ana Mendieta
"I walk beneath . . . imagine me." Sor Juana Ines de Cruz

"Can We Talk Here" is an allusion to Joan Rivers's refrain in her comedic sketches. The poem is loosely based on her jokes.

"Rosy Complexion" is based on the Shanna Compton poem, "Urges in Regard to Which Girls Should Receive Especial Instructions," from her collection *For Girls (& Others): Poems*.

ABOUT THE AUTHOR

Carmen Giménez Smith is the author of a memoir, *Bring Down the Little Birds*, winner of a 2011 American Book Award, and four poetry collections: *Milk and Filth*; *Goodbye, Flicker*; *The City She Was*; and *Odalisque in Pieces*. She teaches in the creative writing programs at New Mexico State University and serves as the editor-in-chief of the literary journal *Puerto del Sol*. She is also the publisher of Noemi Press.